PAGLIACCI

Opera in Two Acts

Words and Music by

Ruggiero Leoncavallo

English Version by
JOSEPH MACHLIS

ED. 2560

G. SCHIRMER, *Inc.*

DISTRIBUTED BY
HAL•LEONARD®
CORPORATION
7777 W. BLUEMOUND RD. P.O. BOX 13819 MILWAUKEE, WI 53213

Note

PAGLIACCI

Ruggiero Leoncavallo (1858-1919) was born in Naples, the son of a magistrate. He received his training at the conservatory of his native city. The struggling young composer gave piano and voice lessons to keep from starving, accompanied café-concerts, and in the latter capacity traveled widely. After many disappointments in his career as an operatic composer, he wrote *Pagliacci* (Clowns) for the publishing house of Sonzogno in Milan. The opera, produced when Leoncavallo was thirty-four years old, brought him international fame.

Pagliacci occupies the same position in Leoncavallo's life as its companion piece, *Cavalleria Rusticana,* does in Mascagni's. Each work represents a solitary success that its composer vainly tried to duplicate in his subsequent operas. Both works, too, mark the trend toward realism (*verismo*) that manifested itself in the Italian lyric theater at the end of the nineteenth century. Under the influence of *verismo,* composers began to favor subjects drawn from the life of the common people, presented in swift-moving dramas characterized by a passionate—at times even savage —intensity.

Pagliacci shows Leoncavallo's operatic gift at its most compelling. The work is enormously helped by the dramatic libretto which the composer himself wrote. The play-within-a-play, in which actors re-enact on the stage a situation that has impinged on their personal lives, is a theme that has attracted numerous dramatists, involving as it does the relationship between make-believe and reality. As a matter of fact Leoncavallo was sued for plagiarism by another author. He defended himself by explaining that he remembered a real case of a murder occurring in a traveling theatrical troupe under circumstances similar to those presented in his opera, his father having been the judge at the trial. The suit was withdrawn.

Pagliacci received its premiere at the Teatro dal Verme in Milan on May 21, 1892. The first American performance took place in New York on June 15, 1893. The work was presented at the Metropolitan Opera House on December 11 of that year, with Nellie Melba singing the role of Nedda, Fernando de Lucia as Canio and Mario Ancona as Tonio.

J.M.

THE STORY

The action takes place in a village in Calabria during the Feast of the Assumption. In the prologue, Tonio appears before the curtain to explain to the audience that the play they are about to see is no fantasy but is, as he says, "a picture of life," presenting the emotions and passions of real men and women.

ACT I. The curtain rises on a little square in a typical Italian village. To the right we see a modest traveling theater. The villagers, dressed in their holiday best, hail the arrival of a troupe of strolling players—especially Canio, "the prince of comedians." Canio, the head of the troupe, urges the crowd to attend the performance to be given that night. He goes off with some of the villagers for a glass of wine at the nearest tavern.

Tonio the hunchback, the clown of the company, remains behind to finish his chores. Finding Canio's wife, Nedda, alone, he takes the liberty of declaring his love for her. She scorns him. When he insists on a kiss, she grabs a whip and strikes him. Cringing with pain, Tonio swears that she will pay dearly for this.

No sooner has Tonio gone off than Silvio appears. He is the young villager with whom Nedda has been having a romance. He tries to persuade her to leave her husband and run away with him. Nedda at first refuses. Ultimately she gives in to Silvio's impassioned pleading. Tonio, on his way to the tavern, catches sight of the lovers and sees his opportunity for revenge: he runs off to fetch Canio. The enraged husband arrives just in time to hear Nedda promise that she will meet Silvio later that night. At Canio's approach Silvio escapes into the woods. Canio demands that Nedda reveal to him the name of her lover. She refuses. Canio, beside himself, is about to kill her when Peppe, another member of the troupe, stops him. Peppe reminds Canio that the villagers are assembling for the performance, and tells Nedda to get dressed for the play. There follows Canio's famous outcry of despair: he must go on the stage as Pagliaccio—the Clown—and make people laugh, even though his heart is breaking.

ACT II. The villagers gather for the play. There is great excitement as they pay admission and find seats. The play presented by Canio and his little troupe centers around the theme that has been a staple item of popular comedy for centuries: the trusting husband deceived by a faithless wife. Tonio plays the part of the stupid servant Taddeo, who declares his love for Columbine (Nedda), only to be scorned by her. Peppe plays the role of Columbine's lover, Harlequin. Their intimate little supper is interrupted by the unexpected arrival of the husband, Pagliaccio (Canio). Harlequin escapes through the window as Nedda promises to meet him later that night, using the same words as she did to Silvio that afternoon. As Canio proceeds to play his part, make-believe gradually retreats before the tragic reality of his situation. He insists that Nedda reveal the name of her lover. She laughs him off and tries to continue the comedy; the audience is amused. But Canio, carried away, reproaches her with her ingratitude and her betrayal. The spectators are deeply moved; some of them begin to wonder whether the actors are playing parts or are in earnest. Nedda reminds Canio that she has never been a coward and persists in her refusal to name the man she loves. Pushed beyond the breaking point, Canio seizes a knife from the table and stabs Nedda. With her last breath she cries out for Silvio, who has been watching the play. He runs to the stage to help her but is too late. Canio, now aware that Silvio was his wife's lover, stabs him to death. Amid the agitation of the horrified onlookers, Canio stands as in a trance and lets the knife fall from his hand, murmuring, "The comedy is ended!"

J.M.

CAST OF CHARACTERS

CANIO, head of a troupe of strolling players (Pagliaccio in the play) . . . Tenor

NEDDA, his wife (Columbine in the play) . . . . Soprano

TONIO, a member of the troupe (Taddeo in the play) . . . . Baritone

PEPPE, a member of the troupe (Harlequin in the play) . . . . Tenor

SILVIO, a villager . . . . Baritone

Peasants and Villagers

PLACE: A village in Calabria, Italy

TIME: In the 1860's

INDEX

Pagliacci
Drama in Two Acts
Prologue

English Version by
JOSEPH MACHLIS

Words and Music by
R. Leoncavallo

45607cx **Orchestra material may be rented from the Publishers.**

4

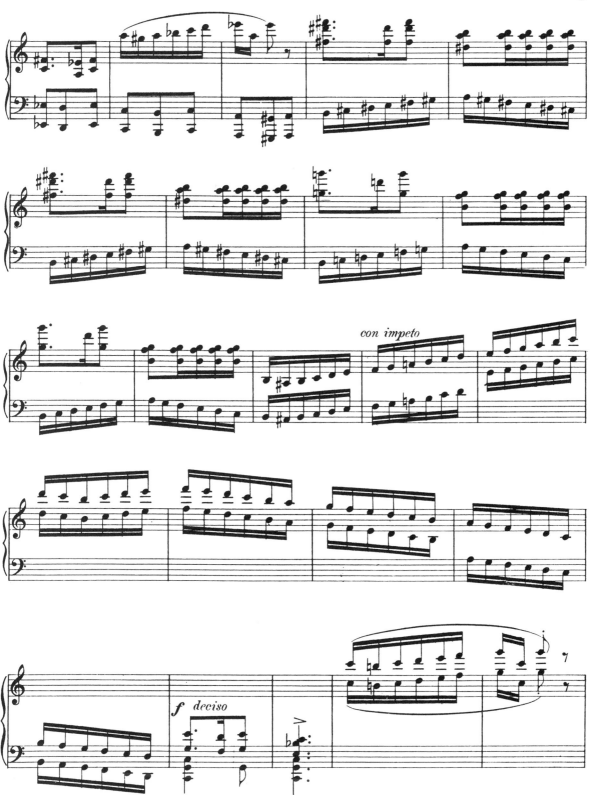

45607

6

7

45607

8

Un po' meno presto che nell' Introd^{ne}($\downarrow$. = 80)

Ma non per dir - - vi co - me pria:
Ma - ny a time peo - ple have said:

a tempo

»Le la - cri - me che noi ver - siam son fal - se!
"The tears that they shed are not real . . . they're act - ing.

De - gli spa - si - mi e de' no - stri mar - tir
And their suf - fer - ing need not move o - ur hearts.

non al - lar - ma - te - vi!«
it but make-be - lieve!"

10

45607

ve - ro i-spi - ra - - va - si.
brings them the na - ked truth.
Un ni - do di me -
One mor - ning as he a -

mo - rie in fon-do a l'a - ni - ma can-ta-va un gior - no,
wak - ened, beau-ti - ful me - mor - ies brought him a vi - sion.
ed
While

e - i con ve - re la - cri - me scris-se, e i sin - ghioz -
writ - ing, he wept with ten - der com - pas-sion, and his po -

zi il tem - po gli bat - - te - - va - no!
em re - leased the grief that filled ___ his heart!

poi - chè siam uo - - mi - ni di car - ne e
We too are men like you, we share hu - man

d'os - - sa, e che di que -
weak - - ness. Just like you, be -

st'or - fa - no mon - do al pa - ri di voi spi - ria - mo
wil - dered and help - less, we go through this lone - ly world in

l'ae - re! Il con - cet - to vi dis - si... Or a - scol-
dark - ness. This the au - thor in - ten - ded. Now see how

45607

Act I
Scene I

Scene. The entrance of a village – where two roads meet. On right a travelling theatre. As the curtain rises, sounds of a trumpet out of tune and a drum are heard. Laughing, shouting, whistling, voices approaching. Enter villagers in holiday attire. Tonio looks up road on left; then, annoyed by the crowd which stares at him, lies down in front of the theatre. Time 3 o'clock. Bright sunlight.

18

gran - di e ra - gaz - zi, ai mot - ti, ai
We greet them glad - ly! Their wit and

Ri - tor - na - no!
They're here a - gain!

qua!
here!

Ten. I

Ten. II

Ri -
They're

laz - zi ap - plau - de o - gnun.
laugh - ter We all ap - plaud.

Ten. I & II

tor - na - no! Ap - plau - de o - gnun.
here a - gain! We all ap - plaud.

Bass II

I & II

Pa - gliac - cio è là! _____
Pa - gliac - cio's here! _____

Pa - gliac - cio è
Pa - gliac - cio's

45607

20

45607

24

45607

32

45607

36

45607

(beating the drum to drown the voices of the crowd)

45607

44

45607

Tonio (aside, as he goes)

(Tonio enters the theatre)

La pa-ghe-ra - - i! bri-gan-te!
He will re-gret this, I swear it!

l.h. *p* *r.h.*

(Four or five villagers approach Canio)

A Villager (to Canio)

Di', con noi vuoi be - ve - re un buon bic-
Say, if you can spare the time, why don't you

chie - re sul - la cro - ce - vi - a? Di', vuoi tu?
have a drink with us at the ta - vern? Come with us!

Canio   Peppe (reappearing)

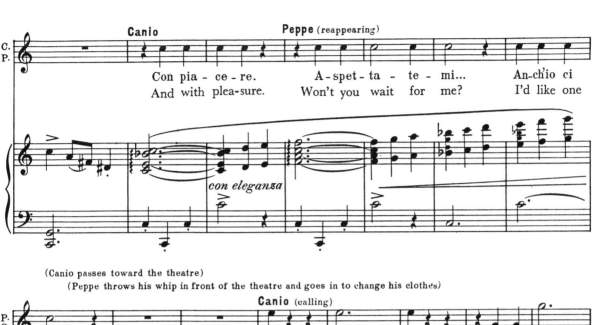

Con pia - ce - re.   A - spet - ta - te - mi...   An-ch'io ci
And with plea-sure.   Won't you wait for me?   I'd like one

(Canio passes toward the theatre)
(Peppe throws his whip in front of the theatre and goes in to change his clothes)

Canio (calling)

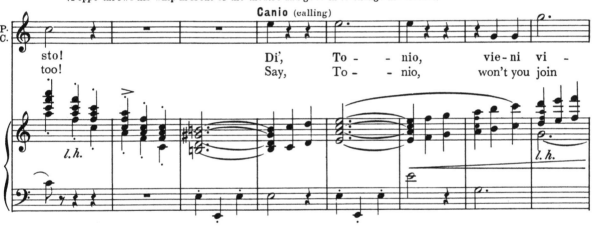

sto!   Di',   To - nio,   vie - ni vi -
too!   Say,   To - nio,   won't you join

Tonio (from within)

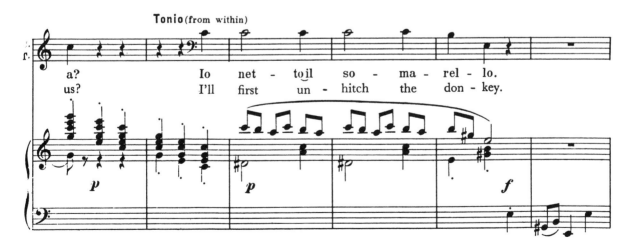

a?   Io   net - to il   so - ma - rel - lo.
us?   I'll   first   un - hitch   the   don - key.

48

Another Villager (jestingly)

Pre - ce - de - te - mi.
Don't you wait for me.

Ba - da, Pa - gliac - cio,
Care - ful, Pa - gliac - cio.

ei so - lo vuol re - sta - re per
He stays be - hind on pur - pose, So

Canio (smiling, but knitting his brows)

far la cor - te a Ned - da!
he can flirt with Ned - da.

Eh! Eh!
Eh! What!

lento

Vi pa - re?
You think so?

p

pp

8va bassa
K. dr.

45607

(Canio approaches Nedda and kisses her forehead)

Scene and Chorus of the Bells

Meno (♩ = 160)

(Oboe within)

Boys

(rushing to the left and looking off)

I zam - po - gna - ri!
Here come the bag-pipes!

Sopr.

Soli I

I zam - po - gna - ri!
Here come the bag-pipes!

Villagers

Bass

Soli I

Ver - so la chie - sa
And now to church, it's

54

45607

45607

58

45607

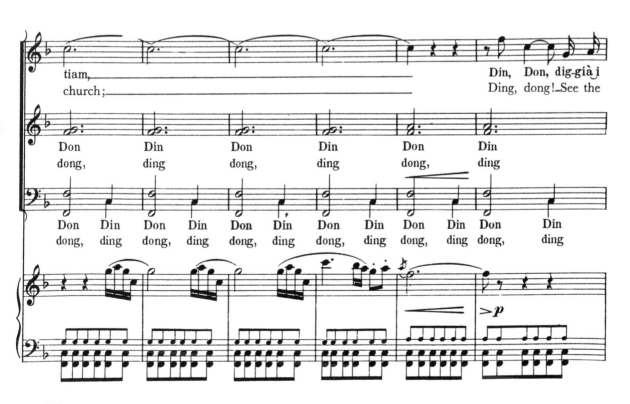

60

45607

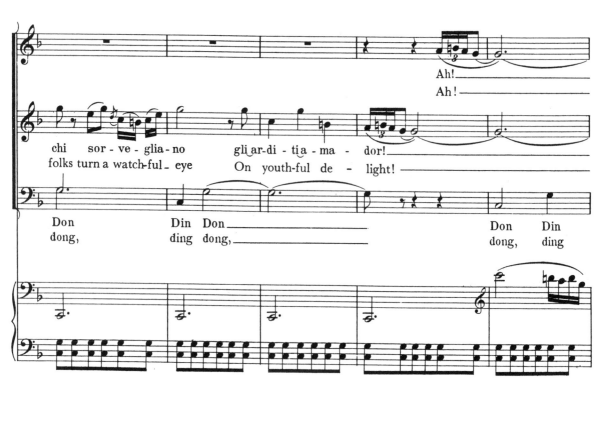

64

45607

(The couples go off by road at back)

66

Scene II (Nedda alone, then Tonio)

(looking to the sky)

Oh! che vo - lo d'au - gel - li,
Ah, you lit - tle birds sing - ing!

e quan - te stri - da!
What love - ly mu - sic!

Che chie - don? do - ve van?
What lures you? Who can say?

chis - sà! La mam - ma mia, che la buo - na ven - tu - ra an-nun-
Who knows? My mo - ther, Who read the fu - ture and knew ma - ny

zia - va,
se - - crets,

com - pren - de - va il lor
Un - der - stood your

can - to   e_a   me bam -   bi - na   co - sì   can -
lan - guage.   When I was   lit - tle,   how her song en -

Ballatella

ta - va: Hui!   Hui!
thralled me: Ah!   Ah!

Vivace (♩.= 66)
in Uno come uno scherzo

pp
bisbigliando

* If the singer wishes to omit the trills, the orchestra goes to the bar marked ℅, skipping one measure

qui   che vo-glio   dir - te - lo,
now   I have to   speak   to you!

e tu m'a - scol - - te - ra - - - - -
And I in - sist   you 'hear

i,   che t'a - - - - mo   e   ti   de -
me: I love   you!   You   are   my

(picks up the whip, and strikes Tonio in the face)

(rushing to catch her)

mi - a!
ter - mined!

Nedda

Poco meno

Mi - se - ra - bi - le!
Don't you dare, you swine!

(screaming and drawing back) *declamato*

Poco meno

ff

a piacere

Per la
By the

a piacere

Ver - gin pia di mez - z'a - go - sto, Ned - da, lo
bles - sed saints and Ho - ly Vir - gin, Ned - da, I

col canto

45607

N. Io mi con-fi-do a te,_____
You are the one I a-dore..._____

N. a te cui die - di_il cor!_____ Non
you are my one de - light!_____ I

N. a - bu - sar di me,_____ del
trust you, dear - est friend,_____ with

f   *p affannoso*

N. mio feb - bri - le a - mor!_____ Non
all my heart and soul!_____ You

f   *p*

If too long, omit from ⊕ to 𝄋, page 107.

45607

110

45607

114

45607

116

45607

Scena and Finale I

(Tonio and Canio appear from the crossroad)

(Canio rushes to the wall, Nedda bars his way. Short struggle; he pushes her aside and leaps over the wall)

Concitato ($\downarrow$ = 120)

45607

120

45607

122

Canio (with suppressed anger)

De-ri-sio-ne e scher-no!   Nul-la! Ei ben lo co-
To be mocked and help-less!   Va-nished! That shows you how

no-sce quel sen-tier.   Fa lo stes-so; poi-chè del dru-do il
well he knows the path.   It does not mat-ter be-cause you're going to

(furiously to Nedda)

Nedda (turning)   Canio (starting in frenzy)

no-me or mi di-rai.   Chi?!   Tu, pel padre e-ter-no!...
tell me Your lov-er's name.   Who?   You, by God in hea-ven!

45607

re - ci - ta. Chis-sà ch'e-gli non ven-ga a lo spet-ta - co-lo
pare the play. Who knows? May-be he'll come to-night to see the show ...

misterioso *calando*

e si tra-di - sca! Or via. Bi - so - gna
And we'll un-mask him! Now come..., you must pre -

sotto voce

Peppe

(Peppe comes from the theatre)
(Tonio goes toward the back)

An-diamo, via,
It's get-ting late.

fin - ge-re per ri - u - scir!
tend a-while, and we'll suc - ceed!

legato il basso e **p** *sempre*

stage, he pushes it roughly, as if not wishing to enter; then, seized by a new

cresc. sempre

fit of sobbing, he again buries his face in his

f

poco rit. con dolore

p

(The curtain begins to fall slowly)

hands; takes three or four steps towards the curtain, from which he had

rianimando

recoiled in fury, and [on these chords] enters and disappears)

rit. ed accentato molto

marcato il canto

r.h.

End of Act I

Intermezzo

Act II

Peppe comes from behind, blowing a trumpet; Tonio follows, beating a big drum, and goes to take up his position on left of theatre. Meantime people come from all directions to the play, and Peppe places benches for the women.

Scene I. Men, Women and Chorus

138

Chorus

Sop. I

(from behind the scene)

Ohè! ____
Oho! ____

Ten. I

Ohè! ____
Oho! ____

ad lib.

Fl.

45607

145

45607

(Silvio comes from back and

takes his place in front on left, nodding to his friends)

148

45607

(Exit Tonio behind theatre, carrying away the big drum. Peppe goes to settle the women who are quarreling about their seats)

150

45607

(Silvio passes on right, seeing Nedda going round with plate for the money, and approaches her)

154

(Nedda walks away, and goes on collecting money)

S.

Non o-bli - ar!
Do not be late!

Sopr. I
Suv - via!
Come here!

Sopr. II
Suv - via!
Come here!

Bass I
Suv -
Come

Bass II
Suv -
Come

Sopr. I

Sopr. II

Ten. I
spic - cia - - - te - vi!
O hur - - - ry up!

Ten. II
spic - cia - - - te - vi!
O hur - - ry up!

Bass I
via, spic - cia - te - vi!
here! It's get - ting late!

Bass II
via, spic - cia - te - vi!
here! It's get - ting late!

45607

(enters theatre, followed by Nedda)

158

45607

162

45607

The Play

SCENE II. The curtain of the Theatre drawn aside. The scene, roughly painted, represents a little room with two side-doors, a practicable window at back, table and two common chairs on right. Nedda, dressed as Columbine.

Tempo di Minuetto (♩ = 69)

(as the curtain opens, Columbine is seated near table; from time to time she

looks anxiously at the door on right)

(Columbine rises, goes to look out of window, and then returns to the front, walking about restlessly)

Columbine

Pa - gliac - cio mio ma - ri -- - to
Pa - gliac - cio, my___ hus - - band,

a tar - da not - te sol ri - tor - ne - rà...
Won't be re - turn - ing till ve - ry late to - night.___

SERENATA

Allegretto un poco moderato ($\quad$=120)

(Columbine, hearing the sound of a guitar off the stage, rushes to window with a cry of joy, but does not open it)

Di___ te chia-man-do, e so_spi_ran_do a-spet-ta il po-ve-rin!___
See,___ I stand a-lone and sigh with long-ing as I wait for you!___

La___
Ah,___

tua fac-cet-ta mo-stra-mi, ch'io vo' ba-ciar sen-za tar-
Won't you show your lit-tle face that I may kiss___ kiss you a-

poco rit.

a tempo

senza respirare

dar___ la tua boc-cuc-cia. A-mor mi
gain!___ O my be-lov-ed, how I a-

a tempo

col canto

45607

170 Tempo di Minuetto (♩= 69)

Columbine (coming down stage)

Di fa-re il se - gno con - ve -
And now he'll give___ me the

nu - to ap - pres - sa l'i - stan - te,
sig - nal. The mo - ment ap - proach - es

ed Ar - lec - chi - no a - spet - ta!
when we will be to - ge - ther!

(Columbine sits down again at table)

Taddeo (Tonio, dressed as Taddeo, peeps thro' door and watches Nedda)

È
Be -

45607

Scena Comica

Andantino sostenuto (♩=76)
con eleganza

Ed an - zi, ec - - - co - ci_en -
Or bet - ter . . . I and the

tram - bi ai pie - di tuo - i!
chick - - en be - fore you kneel - ing.

Poi - chè l'o - ra è suo - na - ta, o Co - lom -
For the hour is u - pon us when I'm re -

bi - na, di sve - lar - ti_il mio cor!
veal - ing All the love in my heart!

Poco più *senza troppo affrett.*

(spectators laugh after Harlequin's speech)

Taddeo

H. fre - sco!
Ta. walk!____ Nu - mi! s'a - - man! m'ar -
Good - ness! They're lo - - vers! I

(to Harlequin)

ren - - do ai det - - ti tuo - - i.
think they'll hard - ly miss me!

(extending his hands) *rit.*

Vi be ne -
Bless you, my

col canto

(retreating toward the door)

di - co! Là ve - glio su vo -
child - ren. Now I'll watch out - - side the

(exit by the door right; the spectators laugh and applaud)

i!____
door.____

p

188

45607

190

45607

196

45607

Movimento di Gavotta come nella Commedia

(going

via, così ter-ri - bi - le dav-ver non ti cre-de - o! Qui nul-la v'ha di tra-gi-co.
you give in to jeal-ous-y I wish that I could cure you! There's nothing here that you need fear

towards the door)

Vie-ni a dir-glio Tad-de - o, che l'uom se - du-to or dianzi, or
Tad - de - o will as-sure you! The one who kept me com-pan-y be-

molto rit. affrett. rit.

dian-zi a me vi - ci - no e - ra... il pau-ro - so ed in - no - cuo Ar-lec-chi-
fore you be-gan to bel-low, He was ... on-ly Har-le-quin, that sweet _ lit-tle fel-

200

45607

206

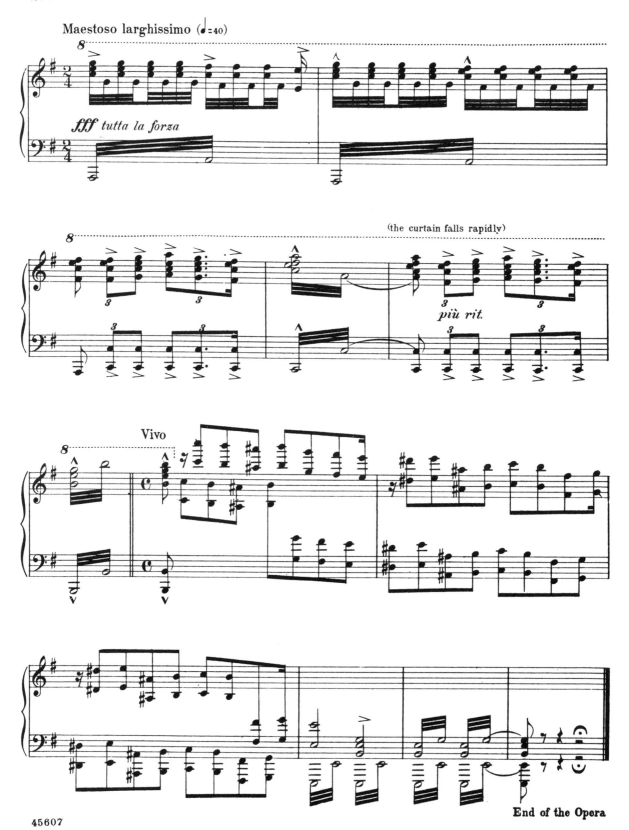

End of the Opera